DEVELOPING A
MARKETING PLAN FOR YOUR BOOK
MADE SIMPLE

DR. ROSIE MILLIGAN

Professional Publishing House   California

Published and Distributed by:
Professional Publishing House
1425 W. Manchester Ave., Suite B
Los Angeles, California 90047
www.professionalpublishinghouse.com
Drrosie@aol.com
(323) 750-3592

Cover design: Jay De Vance, III

First printing: August 2012
10 9 8 7 6 5 4 3 2 1

ISBN: 978-0-9853259-7-8

ABOUT THE AUTHOR

Dr. Rosie Milligan, professional business consultant, publisher, author, financial/estate planner and Ph.D. in Business Administration, has always been an achiever. Every career or business in which she has been involved includes helping others accomplish their goals in life. Her motto, "Erase No, Step Over Can't and Move Forward With Life," has been a motivating influence for hundreds to whom she has been mentor and role model.

Dr. Milligan is an expert in the publishing industry, with thirty years experience. Under her publishing house, Professional Publishing House, she has published more than three hundred titles. Many authors she published were signed by mainstream publishers, and have taken their places on numerous best-seller's lists across the country. Using her expertise, she has set up independent publishing companies for 25 of her clients. Additionally, she assisted Maxine Thompson, a top literary agent in Southern California, launch her literary agency business.

Dr. Milligan has authored seventeen books and co-authored six books. Her books *Starting a Business Made Simple* and *Getting out of Debt Made Simple*, have helped many across the country. She is the author of seventeen books. She has co-authored four books with her sister, Attorney Clara Hunter King, *What You Need To Know Before You Start A Business, Departing This Life Preparations, How To Write A Book Made Simple, and ABC's On How To Prepare Your Manuscript For Editing, Formatting, And Printing*, and *What You Need to Know Before You Get Hitched.*

A successful motivational speaker and trainer, she has appeared on numerous television and radio shows, such as Sally Jesse Raphael in New York; A.M. Philadelphia; Evening Exchange in Washington, D.C., Marilyn Kagan Show in Los Angeles, and she is a regular guest on Stevie Wonder's KJLH Radio. She is the host of a weekly live Internet talk show and she is founder and director of "Black Writers on Tour."

DEVELOPING A
MARKETING PLAN FOR YOUR BOOK
MADE SIMPLE

Writing your marketing plan is as important as writing your book, creating the difference between bestseller and no sales at all. Whether you are independently published or traditionally published, the system of introducing the book to the right audience is truly the difference between failure and success. Without a marketing plan, you are planning to fail.

Book sales do not *just* happen. You must make them happen. Your one book will compete with 2,000 plus titles in the average bookstore and multiple of thousands online. A book does not jump off the shelf. The prospective reader must reach for it, and marketing is what tells them it is there.

A marketing plan must show the revenue streams you expect to reach. This outline will help you, as an author, to meet your income or sales goals. It details the market you are seeking and how you will reach them.

To help you in building the right plan for your book, below is a question and answer approach. Answering these questions will put you on the right track to increased book sales.

WHO WILL BUY MY BOOK?

When you know who will buy your book, you will then know your target market. You must be able to reach directly to the potential reader. Successful marketing begins with identifying the prospect and tactics for reaching that prospect. The book reading market is so huge that it is nearly impossible to wrap your hand around it. When I would ask an author, "Who is your target market?" Often, the response is "Everybody." Not everyone will want to read your book, plan on this. Before you begin to write your book, you should have in mind who are the people, organizations, etc., who are more than likely to want to purchase your book. Next, list the benefits for those whom you think will like to buy your book. A book is like any other product, there must be a demand for the information. The true concept of a business is finding a need and filling it. If there is no need for the information that you are sharing, then its not worth your money spent or effort. You must define, with a very clear picture, who is interested in your book.

Does the reader want or need the book? People are more likely to buy something they need before something they want. The marketing plan must identify the need and benefit for each of your target markets.

Every need you identify points directly to a sales opportunity. You must narrow it down and find a unique angle about your book. You cannot be everything to everyone, but you can target 100% of a specific part!

WHAT IS YOUR MISSION STATEMENT?

Let's say you are writing a book on "How to divorce proof your marriage." Your mission statement may read as such: To empower men/women with vital information needed about marriage before saying "I Do."

What is your GOAL?

Your goal could be to curtail the divorce rate and to prevent children from having to be reared by a single parent.

Pursue Goals That Are Important To You

Your goal may be to help solve a social issue. Your goal may be to sell three million copies. It may be to define or present your knowledge to a certain business or social organization. It may be to keep your job at a university— publish or perish. It may be to help people solve medical problems. Whatever your goals are, they need to be written.

Your goal is part of your mission. It is why you are doing what you are doing. An interesting exercise is to state your goal in five words.

How Do You Plan To Accomplish Your Goals?

This is where your marketing strategy comes into play. I have reviewed many business plans and what they all have in common is a very weak marketing plan. Your marketing plan is the lifeline of the success of the business. Marketing tells what you are going to do to reach your intended target market.

What Is Your Marketing Strategy And What Actions Will You Take?

It starts with your GOALS and everything you do to market your book should be in support of your goals.

Objectives—steps you are able to take to reach your GOAL.

Simple Example:

- Sell 5,000 books in the first three months

- Seek single groups to speak to via church groups and other organizations

- Present a proposal to high schools to have you speak to senior classes.

- Offer church bookstore and beauty shops and barber shop a discount for selling your books

- Identify and approach the bookstore managers. Write a press release about your personal appearances. Create posters for in-store publicity.

- Send your press release to traditional and Internet talk show host

- Send your press release to major television networks.

- Send a press release to local and national newspapers.

- Develop an online blog.

- Ask newspapers to review your book or allow you to write an article or weekly column whereby you can use a by-line

- Develop marketing tools such as: book markers, 2 x 6

- Request to do workshop at your local library.

- Utilize every Social Media available

- Contact your local cable stations about being a guest.

- Develop a speaker's package and contract

- Volunteer to speak at Expos.

- If you have fear of speaking—join a Toastmaster's group

- Develop Marketing Tools such as:

  - Two-sided, full-colored business cards and bookmarks

  - Two-sided, full-colored glossy 4 x 6 post cards (as handouts or postal mailing)

  - Develop full–colored 11 x 17, 24 x 36, and 36 x 48-inch book cover poster

  - Develop full-colored, tri-fold brochures (book cover in center, author's picture on one side and excerpts from book or back cover information on the other side).

- ◆ Real life-size colored poster, 4 to 6 feet on vinyl stand up with full size picture of author, book cover and verbiage. Stand rolls up into carry case, easy for carrying.

- ◆ Go to www.professionalpublishinghouse.com to view samples of marketing tools.

- ◆ Web Development

- ◆ Develop a website designed with traffic tracking

- ◆ Set up an eCommerce account for web site purchases

All of the above, when written down, becomes more than a To Do List—it is your plan. The PLAN outlines your steps to meet your goal through reachable and reasonable objectives.

Evaluate your goal, see what's working and what is not working and do not hesitate to make changes. Make sure that you have given each marketing technique ample time to see results.

It's important to track where your speaking engagements and book sales come from.

DO YOU HAVE THE TIME AND THE BUDGET TO ACCOMPLISH YOUR GOALS? BE REALISTIC ABOUT YOUR TIME AND MONEY.

Remember that the release of a book is the starting point. Marketing is a like a marathon, take steady steps with an occasional sprint, but it is the pace you set for the long run that counts. You have to be consistent. Overnight sensations take years to create.

Time is the only thing that God gives us equally. You bring the energy and the money. Marketing will grind up all three (time, energy and money) at a pace that surprises the pros—every time. Pace yourself. You don't want to end up tired and broke. This is where your plan works for you. You can anticipate your expenses and investment. Your budget needs to consider your objectives, one at a time, and with proper priority, you can schedule your available resources of time and money.

Here are some expenses you should include in your marketing plan:

- Marketing Materials: posters, flyers, postcards, author cards, bookmarks. Develop a real life-size poster so that you will stand out amongst the crowd.

- Press Release: writing and distribution (consider paid reviewer services).

- Advertising: display ads are generally out of reach, but classified ads, online sponsored search, links and banners can be a good value.

- Internet: a web site for the book with a buy button and a blog can be very beneficial. Google Checkout is a great solution for an inexpensive shopping cart.

The media will probably be more interested in you than in your book. They see books like a commodity. They will see you as an expert. Your expertise is more valuable to them for story content. Your book is a reason for them to talk to you.

I wrote this book out of a sincere desire to help people put their knowledge and dreams into print. I, too, have made my mistakes as a publisher, but it is never too late to start over and correctly market and publish your book. There's an old adage that says, "Practice makes perfect," and it holds true only when you are doing it right from the beginning. If you are practicing wrong, then expect the wrong outcome. Now is the time for you to start over and get it right. Although I cannot guarantee success, the principles here are tried and proven.

For more information on writing and publishing, visit www.professionalpublishinghouse.com.

Best of luck to you!

Other Books/eBooks That Will Help You With Your Writing Career

How To Write A Book Made Simple & Your Publishing Options

ABC'c On How To Prepare Your Book For Editing, Formatting And Editing

Nuts And Bolts For The New Author And The New Publisher Made Simple: What You Need To Know To Jump-Start And Sustain Your Writing/Publishing Business

What You Need To Know Before You Start A Business

Where To Purchase These Books and CDs by Dr. Rosie Milligan

www.professionalpublishinghouse.com

www.Drrosie.com

Amazon.Com

Barnesandnobles.com

Classic One Books And Herbs
1425 W. Manchester Ave.
Los Angeles, Calif. 90047
323-750-4114

Where To Purchase Dr. Rosie's EBook

www.professionalpublishinghouse.com

www..Amazon.com

www.Barnesandnoble.com

Information about Black Writers On Tour Writers Conference
go to: www.blackwritersontour.com

www.ingramcontent.com/pod-product-compliance
Lightning Source LLC
Chambersburg PA
CBHW030014040426
42337CB00012BA/780